MW00973779

Guideposts *Prayers for Easter*

Joy—
How blessed we are
as a family to celebrate
the Resurrection of our
Precious Savior. Happy Birthday—
In Him Alone—
I love you
Trish
03-04

Guideposts®

Prayers FOR EASTER

Compiled by Julie K. Hogan

O death, where is thy sting?
O grave, where is thy victory?
Thanks be to God,
which giveth us the victory
through our Lord Jesus Christ.

—1 Corinthians 15:55, 57

IDEALS PUBLICATIONS
NASHVILLE, TENNESSEE

ISBN 0-8249-4605-7

Published by Ideals Publications, A division of Guideposts
535 Metroplex Drive, Suite 250, Nashville, Tennessee 37211
www.idealspublications.com

Caseside printed in the U.S.A. Text printed and bound in Mexico.
Printed by RR Donnelley & Sons.

Library of Congress Cataloging-in-Publication Data on file.

Publisher, Patricia A. Pingry
Art Director, Eve DeGrie
Copy Editor, Amy Johnson
Permissions, Patsy Jay
Research Assistant, Mary P. Dunn
Designed by DeGrie, Kennedy and Associates
Cover photo: White and pink flowering dogwood trees, Greenfield,
Connecticut. William H. Johnson, Johnson's Photography.

ACKNOWLEDGMENTS
BAKEWELL, JOHN. "Immanuel's Praise." Taken from *Beautiful Poems on Jesus.* Compiled by Basil Miller;
published by Beacon Hill Press of Kansas City. Copyright © 1948. CROWELL, GRACE NOLL. "Grant
Us Strength." An excerpt from *Come See a Man* by Grace Noll Crowell. Copyright © 1956 by Abingdon
Press. Used by permission of the publisher. DAVIS, CHESTER M. "An Easter Prayer" from *Prayer Poems.*
Compiled by O. V. and Helen Armstrong; published by Abingdon-Cokesbury Press, 1942.
Reprinted with permission of the author's estate. ELIOT, T. S. "We Thank Thee." An excerpt from
"Choruses from the Rock" from *Collected Poems, 1909-1962.* Copyright © 1964 by T. S. Eliot. Used by
permission of Harcourt, Inc. HUFFMAN, MARGARET ANN. "Easter" from *Family Celebrations, Prayers, Poems,
and Toasts for Every Occasion.* Compiled by June Cotner, Andrews McMeel Publishing, 1999. Used with
permission of the author's estate. KIRK, JAMES G. "Give Us Clean Hearts" from *Meditations for Lent.*
Copyright © 1988 by James G. Kirk. Used by permission of Westminster John Knox Press.
MARSHALL, PETER. "The Coming of Spring," "For This Day," and "Thy Cross." Taken from *The Prayers
of Peter Marshall.* Copyright © 1982 by Catherine Marshall. Used by permission of Baker Book House,
Co. PERRY, SISTER CAROL. "For Constancy" from *Prayers for Every Need, Vol. 1.* Copyright © 2000 by
Guideposts, Carmel, New York 10512. PISANI, CHRISTINE. "A Lenten Prayer" from *Prayers for Every Need,
Vol. 1.* Copyright © 2000 by Guideposts, Carmel, New York 10512. SMALLEY, STEPHEN S. "Intercede
for Us" from *The Complete Book of Christian Prayer.* Copyright © 1995 by Continuum International
Publishing Group, Inc. Used by permission of the publisher. Our sincere thanks to the following
authors whom we were unable to locate: Karl Barth for "The Easter Light"; Charles Henry Brent for
"Before the Cross"; W. E. Orchard for "On Easter Day"; F. J. Paradise for "Come to Us Now"; Sister
Judith Marie Saenz for "Enter, O Lord"; Nancy Byrd Turner for "Bless Us, Lord."

10 8 6 4 2 1 3 5 7 9

CONTENTS *Prayers for Easter*

PRAYERS FOR LENT

You are washed,

you are sanctified,

you are justified

in the name of the Lord Jesus,

and by the Spirit of our God.

— 1 Corinthians 6:11

Ash Wednesday

O God, we recall that
we are only dust and ashes,
and it is through your grace
that we have been born in baptism
to new life in our
Lord Jesus Christ.
During these forty days,
let us reflect on our lives
in prayer, through penance,
and in the practice of charity,
so that we may then come
to the Easter Day
ready to renew once more
our life-giving
baptism commitment.
We ask this through our
Lord and Saviour
Jesus Christ.

—Author Unknown

Give Us Charity

O Lord, give us more charity,
more self-denial, more likeness to thee.
Teach us to sacrifice
our comforts to others,
and our likings
for the sake of doing good.
Make us kindly in thought,
gentle in word, generous in deed.
Teach us that it is
better to give than to receive,
better to forget ourselves
than to put ourselves forward,
better to minister
than to be ministered unto.
And to thee, the God of love,
be all glory and praise,
now and forever.

—*Henry Alford*

We Thank You

We thank you, Father,
for those days in the desert
when, through prayer and fasting,
Jesus discovered your will for his life
and overcame the temptations
of the evil one.
Help us, during these days of Lent,
to come close to you
and to listen to your voice.
Give us strength
to overcome the temptation
to please ourselves
and live life without you.
Teach us your way,
For Jesus' sake.
Christ give us grace
to grow in holiness,
to deny ourselves,
take up our cross and follow him.

—*from The Alternative Service Book*

Prayer for Strength

O God, who before the Passion
of thine only begotten Son
didst reveal his glory
upon the holy mountain:
grant unto us thy servants,
that in faith beholding
the light of his countenance,
we may be strengthened to bear the cross
and be changed into his likeness
from glory to glory;
through the same Jesus Christ our Lord.

—*Author Unknown*

Give Us Strength

Lord, you, who throughout these forty days
For us did fast and pray,
Teach us to overcome our sins
And close by you to stay.

As you with Satan did contend,
And did the vict'ry win,
O give us strength in you to fight,
In you to conquer sin.

As you did hunger and did thirst,
So teach us, gracious Lord,
To die to self, and so to live
By your most holy word.

And through these days of penitence,
And through your Passiontide,
For evermore, in life and death,
O Lord! with us abide.

Abide with us, that through this life
Of doubts and hope and pain,
An Easter of unending joy
We may at last attain!

—*Claudia F. Hernaman*

Have Mercy, O God

Have mercy upon me, O God,
according to thy lovingkindness:
according unto the multitude
of thy tender mercies
blot out my transgressions.
Wash me thoroughly from mine iniquity,
and cleanse me from my sin.
For I acknowledge my transgressions:
and my sin is ever before me.
Against thee, thee only, have I sinned,
and done this evil in thy sight:
that thou mightest be justified when thou
speakest, and be clear when thou judgest. . . .
Hide thy face from my sins,
and blot out all mine iniquities.
Create in me a clean heart, O God;
and renew a right spirit within me.
Cast me not away from thy presence;
and take not thy holy spirit from me.
Restore unto me the joy of thy salvation;
and uphold me with thy free spirit.

—Psalm 51:1-4, 9-12

Give Us Clean Hearts

Gracious God,
you brought Christ into the world
to bear our afflictions,
and by his stripes we are healed;
we come with thanksgiving
for his cleansing redemption.
Purge the stain of sin within us
and give us clean hearts,
that we may serve you more faithfully.
Renew right minds that we may enjoy
the fruits of your Spirit
and abound in the love, joy, peace,
goodness, and faithfulness we find
in the reconciling love
of Christ Jesus,
our Saviour and Lord.

—*James G. Kirk*

Prayer for Mercy

Almighty and most merciful Father,
we have erred and strayed from thy ways. . . .
We have followed too much
the devices and desires of our own hearts.
We have offended against thy holy laws.
We have left undone those things
which we ought to have done,
and we have done those things
which we ought not to have done. . . .
Spare thou them, O God,
which confess their faults.
Restore thou them that are penitent,
according to thy promises
declared unto mankind
in Christ Jesus our Lord.
And grant, O most merciful Father,
for his sake, that we may hereafter live
a godly, righteous, and sober life,
to the glory of thy holy name.

—from the Book of Common Prayer

I Turn

O immeasurable love!
O gentle love!
Eternal fire!
You are that fire
ever blazing,
O high eternal Trinity.
You are direct
without any twisting,
genuine without any duplicity,
open without any pretense.
Turn the eye of your mercy
on your creatures.
I know that mercy
is your hallmark,
and no matter where I turn
I find nothing
but your mercy.

—*Saint Catherine of Siena*

For Constancy

God, I waver so often.
I make good resolutions,
then I forget them
or make excuses.
Help me this Lent
to become constant
in my desire to have you
at the center of my life.

—Sister Carol Perry

Let Me Hold Fast

Let me hold fast to you,
beautiful Lord,
whom the angels themselves
yearn to look upon.
Wherever you go,
I will follow you.
If you pass through fire,
I will not flinch;
I fear no evil
when you are with me.
You carry my griefs,
because you grieve
for my sake.
You pass through
the narrow doorway
from death to life,
to make it wide enough
for all to follow.
Nothing can ever now separate
me from your love.

—*Bernard of Clairvaux*

A Lenten Prayer

O God, I so want to draw closer
to you this Lent.
Please help me see you more clearly,
hear you more distinctly,
and follow you more intentionally
during these next forty days.
Give me peace of mind and heart
and the will to push
all unnecessary things
to the periphery of my life.

Thank you for this opportunity
to come closer to you
on my spiritual path.
Bless me in this endeavor, I pray,
and help me keep from
backsliding in the process.
I wait on you,
God of my understanding.

—Christine Pisani

Blend Our Wills

O Lord Jesus Christ,
the same yesterday,
today, and forever;
O Saviour of the ever-loving heart;
we have grieved and wounded thee.
By our wilfulness,
by our moral cowardice,
by our thoughtlessness,
by our self-seeking
we share in crucifying thee afresh.
By the revelation thou hast made
of eternal love,
help us to enter
into the travail of thy soul;
and by loving self-sacrifice,
blend our wills with thy will
to bring all men
to a knowledge of the Father.
Amen.

—Author Unknown

Give Me Grace

Give me grace, O my Father,
to be utterly ashamed
of my own reluctance.
Rouse me from sloth and coldness,
and make me desire you
with my whole heart.
Teach me to love meditation,
sacred reading, and prayer.
Teach me to love
that which must
engage my mind
for all eternity.

—*John Henry Newman*

Trespass

I offer you prayers
for all whom
I have grieved,
vexed and oppressed,
by word or deed,
knowingly
or unknowingly,
that you might
equally forgive
all of us our sins,
and all of us
our offenses
against each other.

—*Thomas à Kempis*

Abide with Me

O my God,
my whole life has been a course
of mercies and blessings,
shown to one who
has been most unworthy of them.
Year after year
thou hast carried me on,
removed dangers from my path,
refreshed me,
borne with me,
directed me,
sustained me.
O forsake me not,
when my strength faileth me.
And thou wilt never forsake me.
I may securely repose upon thee.
While I am true to thee,
thou wilt still,

and to the end,
be superabundantly good to me.
I may rest upon thy arm;
I may go to sleep in thy bosom.
Only give me, and increase in me,
that true loyalty to thee,
which is the bond of the covenant
between thee and me,
and the pledge
in my own heart and conscience
that thou, the Supreme God,
wilt not forsake me.
Amen.

—John Henry Newman

We Beseech Thee

We beseech thee,
good Lord,
that it may please thee
to give us true repentance:
to forgive us all our sins,
negligences,
and ignorances;
and to imbue us
with the grace
of thy Holy Spirit,
to amend our lives
according to thy holy word.

—Archbishop Thomas Cranmer

With All Our Heart

O God,
who wouldest not
the death of a sinner,
but that he should be converted
and live:
forgive the sins
of us who turn to thee
with all our heart,
and grant us the grace
of eternal life,
through Jesus Christ
our Lord.

— *Early Scottish Prayer*

PRAYERS FOR HOLY WEEK

For God so loved the world,

that he gave his only begotten Son,

that whosoever believeth in him

should not perish,

but have everlasting life.

— John 3:16

Ride On

Jesus, King of the universe,
Ride on in humble majesty:

Lord, this Palm Sunday
may we recognize in you
the Lord who comes to his world,
and join with full heart in the children's "hosannas."

Ride on, through conflict and debate,
Ride on, through prayer and betrayal:

Lord, this Palm Sunday
forgive me my evasions of truth . . .
my weakness which leaves me sleeping
even while in others you suffer and are anguished;
my cowardice that does not risk
the consequences of publicly acknowledging
you as Lord.

Ride on to the empty tomb
  and your rising in triumph,
Ride on to raise up your church,
  a new body for your service;
Ride on, King Jesus,
  to renew the whole earth in your image.
In compassion come to help us.

—*Author Unknown*

Glory, Laud, Honor

All glory, laud, and honor
To you, Redeemer, King!
To whom the lips of children
Made sweet hosannas ring.

You are the King of Israel,
And David's royal Son,
Now in the Lord's Name coming,
Our King and Blessed One.

The company of angels
Are praising you on high;
And mortals, joined with all things
Created, make reply.

The people of the Hebrews
With palms before you went:
Our praise and prayers and anthems
Before you we present.

To you before your passion
They sang their hymns of praise:
To you, now high exalted,
Our melody we raise.

Their praises you accepted,
Accept the prayers we bring,
Great source of love and goodness,
Our Saviour and our King.

—*Theodulf of Orleans*

King of Glory

O Christ, the King of glory,
who didst enter the holy city
in meekness
to be made perfect through
the suffering of death:
give us grace, we beseech thee,
in all our life here
to take up our cross daily
and follow thee,
that hereafter
we may rejoice with thee
in thy heavenly kingdom;
who livest and reignest
with the Father and the Holy Spirit,
world without end.

—*Author Unknown*

Triumph

Jesus, you rode into your city
in triumph on this day,
receiving the shouts
and the welcome of many.
Come into this church today.
Receive our welcome and our acclaim.
Come to rule in the hearts and minds
of all who lead our worship
and then help us all to go out
and to proclaim you
as King over all the world
and every life.
Dear Master, we remember that many
who claimed you as King on Sunday
shouted "Crucify" on Friday.
So confirm our faith today,
that our love for you will never falter
or turn to hatred, but will remain
constant now and forever.
We offer our worship to you,
Lord, with all our love. Amen.

—*from Prayers before Worship*

Entering Jerusalem

Let the mountains and all the hills
break out into great rejoicing
at the mercy of God,
and let the trees of the forest
clap their hands.
Give praise to Christ,
all nations,
magnify him,
all peoples, crying:
glory to thy power, O Lord.
Seated in heaven upon thy throne
and on earth upon a foal,
O Christ our God,
thou hast accepted the praise of angels
and the songs of the children
who cried out to thee:
blessed art thou that comest
to call back Adam.

—*Author Unknown*

Grant Us Grace

O Lord God,
whose blessed Son, our Saviour,
gave his back to the smiters
and hid not his face from shame;
Grant us grace
to take joyfully
the sufferings of the present time,
in full assurance of the glory
that shall be revealed;
through the same thy Son
Jesus Christ our Lord.
Amen.

—from The Book of Common Prayer

Assist Us, Lord

Assist us mercifully
with thy help,
O Lord God
of our salvation;
that we may enter with joy
upon the meditation
of those mighty acts,
whereby thou hast given unto us
life and immortality;
through Jesus Christ
our Lord.
Amen.

—from The Book of Common Prayer

Mealtime Prayer

God our Father,
our family is gathered here
to share in this meal.
On the night before he died,
your son Jesus gathered
his followers around him
and shared a meal with them
as a sign of his love for them.
Help us to always
love one another,
for we know that
where there is charity
and love,
you are there also.
Bless us, our food,
and all our works
in the name of your son, Jesus.
Amen.

—Author Unknown

Last Supper

Lord Jesus Christ,
who, when thou wast able
to institute thy holy sacrament
at the Last Supper,
didst wash the feet of the apostles,
and teach us,
by thy example,
the grace of humility:

Cleanse us, we beseech thee,
from all stain of sin,
that we may be worthy partakers
of thy holy mysteries;
who livest and reignest with the Father
and the Holy Ghost,
one God, world without end.

—Church of England

Intercede for Us

Lord Christ,
our Servant and Saviour,
on earth you washed
the feet of your disciples,
and now through your cross
and resurrection
you always live
to make intercession for us:
give us grace
to be your faithful disciples
and servants to our lives' end;
for your name's sake.

—Stephen S. Smalley

Charity and Love

Where charity and love are, there is God.
The Love of Christ has gathered us as one.
Let us rejoice and be glad in him.
Let us fear and love the living God,
And in purity of heart let us love one another.

Where charity and love are, there is God.
When therefore we are gathered together
Let us not be divided in spirit.
Let bitter strife and discord cease between us;
Let Christ our God be present in our midst.

Where charity and love are, there is God.
With all the blessed may we see forever
Thy face in glory, Jesus Christ our God.
Joy that is infinite and undefiled
For all the ages of eternity.

—from the Latin, Ubi Caritas

Restore Us, O God

Grant, we beseech you,
almighty God,
that we, who amid
so many adversities,
do fail through
our own infirmities,
may be restored
through the Passion
and Intercession
of your only begotten Son,
who lives and reigns
with you and the Holy Ghost,
ever one God,
world without end.
Amen.

—from The Common Service Book

Gethsemane

Lord Jesus, you have shaped our faith
by making us believe
you shared our mortal nature.
In Gethsemane
real drops of sweat
fell from your body.

Lord Jesus, you have given us hope,
because you endured
all the spiritual and physical hardships
which mortal nature can suffer.
In Gethsemane
your soul was in torment,
and your heart shook
at the prospect of the
physical pain to come.
You showed all the natural
weaknesses of the flesh,
that we might know
that you have truly
borne our sorrows.

—Saint Bonaventura

He Suffered!

"He suffered!" Was it, Lord, indeed for me,
The Just One for the unjust, thou didst bear
The weight of sorrow that I hardly dare
To look upon, in dark Gethsemane?

"He suffered!" Thou, my near and
  gracious Friend,
And yet my Lord, my God!
  Thou didst not shrink
For me that full and fearful cup to drink,
Because thou lovedst even to the end!

"He suffered!" Saviour, was thy love so vast
That mysteries of unknown agony,
Even unto death, its only gauge could be,
Unmeasured as the fiery depths it passed?

Lord, by the sorrows of Gethsemane
Seal thou my quivering love forever unto thee.

—Frances Ridley Havergal

Grant Us Strength

Dear Jesus,
our hearts are wrung
at the memory of thy suffering,
at the injustice thou didst endure.
Grant that from that awful hour
we may draw strength
from thy strength
for whatever Gethsemane
that may be ours.
May we be able to walk
in the will of God,
out of the darkness
of any night.
Amen.

—*Grace Noll Crowell*

Grant, O Lord

Grant, O Lord,
that in your wounds
I may find my cure,
in your pain my peace,
in your Cross my victory,
in your Resurrection my triumph,
and a crown of righteousness
in the glories
of your eternal kingdom.

—Jeremy Taylor

Good Friday Prayer

Lord Jesus,
who on this holy day
of thy Passion
didst stretch out thine arms
upon the hard wood of the cross,
that all men might be brought
within their saving embrace;
draw us unto thyself
with the bands of thy love,
that we may be found of thee
and find thee;
and grant that,
evermore being bound unto thee
as thy faithful servants,
we may take up our cross daily
and follow thee,
and at last attain to thine eternal joy;
who livest and reignest with the Father
and the Holy Spirit,
world without end.

—Author Unknown

The Foot of the Cross

From the foot of the cross
I look up to thee,
O Lord Jesus,
bow down to me.
For I stand in the faith
of my God today,
Put love in my heart
and hope alway.

—*Author Unknown*

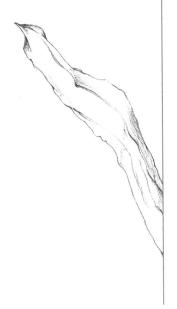

Before the Cross

Saviour, who in human flesh
  conquered tears by crying,
  pain by suffering,
  death by dying,
  we, your servants,
  gather before the Cross
  to commemorate your Passion
  and to contemplate anew
  the wonder of
  your compassionate love.
  As we listen to your gracious words,
  uttered with dying lips,
  illumine our souls
  that we may know the truth,
  melt our hearts
  that we may hate our sins,
  nerve our wills
  that we may do your bidding,
  to the glory of your name
  and our own eternal gain.

—*Charles Henry Brent*

At Nine O'Clock

O Lord Jesus Christ,
son of the living God,
who from the bosom of the Father
didst descend from the heavens to the earth,
and on the wood of the cross
didst suffer five wounds,
and shed thy precious blood
for the remission of our sins:
we meekly beseech thee that,
in the day of judgment,
we may be set on thy right hand,
and hear thy joyful sentence,
"Come, ye blessed of my Father,
enjoy ye the kingdom prepared for you
from the foundation of the world";
where with the Father and the Holy Ghost
thou livest and reignest for ever and ever.

—*John Hilsey*

PRAYERS FOR HOLY WEEK

51

At Noon

O Lord Jesus Christ,
Son of the living God,
who, at the sixth hour of the day,
didst with great tumult
ascend on Golgotha
the Cross of pain;
whereon, thirsting for our salvation,
thou didst permit gall and vinegar
to be given thee to drink:
we beseech thee that thou wouldst
kindle and inflame our hearts
with the love of thy Passion,
and make us to find our delight
in thee alone, our crucified Lord;
who livest and reignest,
world without end.

—John Hilsey

At Three O'Clock

Hear us,
O merciful Lord Jesus Christ,
and remember now the hour
in which thou didst
commend thy blessed spirit
into the hands of thy heavenly Father;
and so assist us by this
thy most precious death,
that, being dead unto the world,
we may live only unto thee;
and that, at the hour
of our departing
from this mortal life,
we may be received
into thine everlasting kingdom,
there to reign with thee,
world without end.

—*John Cosin*

Thy Cross

As we look upon Thy Cross, O Christ,
filled with wonder and with awe
at the love that brought thee to it,
humbly we confess that we have no offering
meet for such a love,
no gift fit for such a sacrifice.
Thou wert willing to go to the Cross
so that men might forever be haunted
by its sign, might return
to the foot of that Cross
to be melted and broken down
in the knowledge of Thy love for us
and all men everywhere.
When we see a love like that—
the love of God
yearning for the hearts of His children,
we know that only love can respond.
We acknowledge, O Lord, that there is
so little in us that is lovable.
So often we are not lovely in our thoughts,
in our words, or in our deeds.

And yet Thou dost love us still,
with a love that neither ebbs nor flows,
a love that does not grow weary,
but is constant—year after year, age after age.
O God, may our hearts be opened
to that love today.
With bright skies above us,
the fields and woods and garden
bursting with new life and beauty,
how can we fail to respond?
With the clear notes of birdsongs
challenging us to praise,
with every lowly shrub and blooming tree
catching new life and beauty,
our hearts indeed would proclaim Thee Lord,
and we would invite Thee to reign over us
and make us truly Thine own.
May Thy healing love invade our inmost
hearts, healing sorrow, pain,
frustration, defeat, and despair.

—*Peter Marshall*

This Night

This is the night,
when Christ broke the bonds
of death and hell,
and rose victorious from the grave.
How wonderful
and beyond our knowing, O God,
is your mercy and lovingkindness to us,
that to redeem a slave,
you gave a Son.
How holy is this night,
when wickedness is put to flight,
and sin is washed away.
It restores innocence to the fallen
and joy to those who mourn.
It casts out pride and hatred
and brings peace and concord.

How blessed is this night, when earth
and heaven are joined
and man is reconciled to God.

Holy Father, accept our evening sacrifice,
the offering of this candle in your honor.
May it shine continually
to drive away all darkness.
May Christ, the Morning Star
who knows no setting,
find it ever burning,
he who gives his light to all creation,
and who lives and reigns
for ever and ever.
Amen.

—*from the Book of Common Prayer*

PRAYERS FOR EASTER DAY

Jesus said unto her, I am the resurrection,

and the life: he that believeth in me,

though he were dead, yet he shall live:

And whosoever liveth and believeth

in me shall never die.

—John 11:25-26

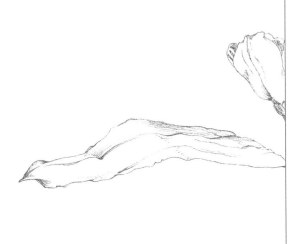

Our Victorious Saviour

O God, you have glorified
our victorious Saviour
with a visible, triumphant Resurrection
from the dead, and ascension into heaven,
where he sits at your right hand;
grant, we beg you,
that his triumphs and glories
may ever shine in our eyes,
to make us more clearly
see through his sufferings,
and more courageously endure our own;
being assured by his example,
that if we endeavor to live and die like him,
for the advancement of your love
in ourselves and others,
you will raise our dead bodies again,
and conforming them to his glorious body,
call us above the clouds,
and give us possession
of your everlasting kingdom.

—*John Wesley*

We Thank Thee

Therefore we thank Thee
for our little light,
that is dappled with shadow.
We thank Thee
who has moved us
to building,
to finding,
to forming
at the ends of our fingers
and beams of our eyes.
And when we have built an altar
to the Invisible Light,
we may set thereon
the little lights
for which our bodily vision
is made.

—*T. S. Eliot*

For This Day

We thank Thee
for the beauty of this day,
for the glorious message
that all nature proclaims:
the Easter lilies with their waxen throats
eloquently singing the good news;
the birds, so early this morning,
impatient to begin their song;
every flowering tree, shrub,
and flaming bush,
a living proclamation from Thee.
O open our hearts
that we may hear it too!

Lead us, we pray Thee,
to the grave that is empty,
into the garden of the Resurrection
where we may meet our risen Lord.
May we never again live
as if Thou were dead!

In Thy presence restore
our faith, our hope, our joy.
Grant to our spirits
refreshment, rest, and peace.
Maintain within our hearts
an unruffled calm,
an unbroken serenity
that no storms of life
shall ever be able to take from us.
From this moment,
O living Christ, we ask Thee
to go with us wherever we go;
be our Companion in all that we do.
And for this greatest of all gifts,
we offer Thee
our sacrifices of thanksgiving.
Amen.

—Peter Marshall

Redemption

O God,
who by thine only begotten Son
hast overcome death
and opened unto us
the gate of everlasting life;
grant, we beseech thee,
that those who have been
redeemed by his Passion
may rejoice in his Resurrection;
through the same
Christ our Lord.
Amen.

—from the Gelasian Sacramentary

An Easter Prayer

O Crucified Son of God, I pray
All hate and evil in me slay.
That I may live with spirit free
Not unto self, but unto thee.

Risen, living, triumphant Lord,
Breathe in my soul thy living word,
That risen, I may walk with thee,
Within appointed paths for me.

Ascended now upon thy throne
Thou wilt not leave us here alone.
Holy Spirit, walk by our side
And bless us on this Eastertide.

—*Chester M. Davis*

Easter Miracle

The moment we have longed for has come;
the night of our desires is here.
What greater occupation could there be
than for us to proclaim
the power of your Resurrection!
This was the night when you shattered
the gates of hell, and you took up
the victory banner of heaven.
This was the night
when you set us among the stars.
When your mother Mary gave birth to you,
she was overwhelmed with joy at your beauty.
Now we are overwhelmed with joy
at your power.
The blood which flowed from your side
has washed away our sins.
Your body rising from the tomb
has promised us eternal life.
Eternal are the blessings
which in your love you have poured upon us.

—from the Gelasian Sacramentary

Be Joyful, Mary

Be joyful, Mary, heav'nly Queen.
Be joyful, Mary!
Your grief is changed to joy serene, Alleluia!
Rejoice, rejoice, O Mary!

The Son you bore by heaven's grace.
Be joyful, Mary!
Did by his death our guilt erase, Alleluia!
Rejoice, rejoice, O Mary!

The Lord has risen from the dead.
Be joyful, Mary!
He rose in glory as he said, Alleluia!
Rejoice, rejoice, O Mary!

Then pray to God, O virgin fair.
Be joyful, Mary!
That he our souls to heaven bear, Alleluia!
Rejoice, rejoice, O Mary!

—from the Latin, Regina Caeli

Christ, Our Example

Lamb of God, I look to thee;
Thou shalt my example be;
Thou art gentle, meek, and mild;
Thou wast once a little child.

Fain I would be as thou art;
Give me thy obedient heart!
Thou art pitiful and kind;
Let me have thy loving mind!

Meek and lowly may I be;
Thou art all humility!
Let me to my betters bow;
Subject to thy parents thou.

Let me above all fulfill
God my heavenly Father's will;
Never his good Spirit grieve;
Only to his glory live!

Thou didst live to God alone;
Thou didst never seek thine own;
Thou thyself didst never please;
God was all thy happiness.

Loving Jesu, gentle Lamb,
In thy gracious hands I am;
Make me, Saviour, what thou art!
Live thyself within my heart!

I shall then shew forth thy praise;
Serve thee all my happy days;
Then the world shall always see
Christ, the Holy Child, in me.

—*Charles Wesley*

An Easter Litany

O God, who art Lord
over all and within all,
teach our hearts to sing for joy
when our lips sing praises unto thee
for all thy mercies.
Banish from our souls, we pray thee,
gloom, discontent, and fear;
and make thy love of us and our love of thee
be in us joy, confidence, and full satisfaction.
Grant us, O Lord, to rest in thee,
and in thee to have our hearts at peace.

O God, who has made us
thy children, and heirs of eternal life,
grant that having this hope
we may purify ourselves,
and become worthy of what thou hast
in keeping for us.
Blessed are the pure in heart, for they shall see thee.

On this day which celebrates
the power of the soul to outlast

the changes of earth,
and to rise victorious
over the bondage of death,
may our immortal being hear the call
and feel its meaning.
Help us to rise from the death of sin to the life of righteousness.

Make us to know, and feel,
that all thy children
are precious in thy sight,
and that they live evermore unto thee.
There shall be no more death;
and thou shalt wipe away all tears from our eyes.
All glory be to thee, O God,
whose light hath shined in our hearts
to show us a way of everlasting life.
Blessed art thou for this light which no darkness overspreads.

Thou art the Lord, who hast shown us such light.
*Thy mercy is everlasting, and thy truth endureth from generation
to generation. Amen.*

—Author Unknown

On Easter Day

O thou who makes the stars
and turnest the shadow of death
into the morning,
on this day of days our hearts exult
with heavenly joy.

We praise thee, our Lord and King,
for the resurrection of the springtime,
for the everlasting hopes that rise
within the human breast,
and for the Gospel which has brought
life and immortality to light.

Receive our thanksgiving,
reveal thy presence,
and send forth into our hearts
the Spirit of the Risen Christ.
Amen.

—*W. E. Orchard*

Come to Us Now

Blessed Christ,
who in this glad and memorable day
didst first fulfill thy promise
of thy presence with thine own,
revealing thyself as alive to those
who mourned thee as dead:

Come to us now,
find the secret way
to all our hearts,
lift the pierced hands
in benediction over us,
breathe upon us the peace
that thou alone canst give.
Amen.

—F. J. Paradise

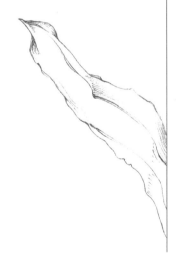

Easter

I have an Easter house today;
The winter's grime is washed away,
My chairs and tables burnished bright,
My mirrors giving back the light;

And roses, fresh from nature's loom,
In springtime beauty and perfume,
Work miracles in every room.

Have I an Easter heart today?
No litter left, no cobwebs grey?
The corner swept so clean and bright
My Lord therein may find delight?

O Christ, new risen from the tomb,
Come, Rose of Sharon, fill each room
Of this poor heart with sweetest bloom.

—Mary Hoge Wardlaw

Bless Us, Lord

In a sweet springtime,
Half the world away,
Jesus Christ arose for us
At the break of day.

Now again it's springtime—
Bending low we pray:
Bless us, Lord of Easter,
On thy Easter Day!

—*Nancy Byrd Turner*

The True Light

Christ, whose glory fills the skies,
Christ, the true and only light,
Sun of righteousness, arise,
Triumph o'er the shades of night;
Dayspring from on high, be near;
Daystar, in my heart appear.

Dark and cheerless is the morn
Unaccompanied by thee;
Joyless is the day's return,
Till thy mercy's beams I see,
Till they inward light impart,
Glad my eyes, and warm my heart.

Visit then this soul of mine,
Pierce the gloom of sin and grief;
Fill me, radiancy divine,
Scatter all my unbelief;
More and more thyself display,
Shining to the perfect day.

—Charles Wesley

The Coming of Spring

We give Thee thanks
for the loveliness of spring
with its promise of summer.
Bird and blossom seem to tell us
of the possibility of new life
for our own souls.
This spring day speaks to us
of beginning again, of new beauty
that can come to reburnish
our own barren lives.
O Lord Jesus, may that transformation
begin in us now as we sit before Thee—
penitent and expectant.
Amen.

—Peter Marshall

PRAYERS FOR EASTER DAY

Guide Me Ever

Guide me ever, great Redeemer,
Pilgrim through this barren land.
I am weak, but you are mighty;
Hold me with your pow'rful hand.
Bread of heaven, bread of heaven,
Feed me now and evermore,
   Feed me now and evermore.

Open now the crystal fountain
Where the healing waters flow;
Let the fire and cloudy pillar
Lead me all my journey through.
Strong deliv'rer, strong deliv'rer,
Shield me with your mighty arm,
   Shield me with your mighty arm.

When I tread the verge of Jordan,
Bid my anxious fears subside;
Bear me thro' the swelling current,
Land me safe on Canaan's side.
Songs of praises, songs of praises,
I will raise forevermore,
   I will raise forevermore.

—*William Williams*

Eternal Praise to You

Eternal praise to you,
my Lord Jesus Christ,
for the time you endured on the cross
the greatest torments
and sufferings for us sinners.
The sharp pain of your wounds
fiercely penetrated even to your blessed soul
and cruelly pierced
your most sacred heart till finally
you sent forth your spirit in peace,
bowed your head,
and humbly commended yourself
into the hands of God your Father;
and your whole body
remained cold in death.

Blessed may you be, my Lord Jesus Christ.
For our salvation you allowed
your side and heart
to be pierced with a lance and from that side
water and your precious blood
flowed out abundantly for our redemption.

Unending honor be to you,
my Lord Jesus Christ.
On the third day you rose from the dead
and appeared to those you have chosen.
And after forty days
you ascended into heaven
before the eyes of many witnesses
and then in heaven
you gathered together in glory
those you love, whom you had freed from hell.

Rejoicing and eternal praise be to you,
my Lord Jesus Christ,
who sent the Holy Spirit
into the hearts of your disciples
and increased the boundless love
of God in their spirits.
Blessed are you, praiseworthy
and glorious forever,
my Lord Jesus.

—*Saint Birgitta*

Easter

Dear God, today we celebrate
the triumph of light over dark,
day over night,
truth over lie.

We'll take this message with us
into the uncertainties of tomorrow,
hearing your promise
in the songs of birds
who begin singing again
before the storm has fully ended.

They know all along
that clouds cover,
not banish,
the sun.

—*Margaret Anne Huffman*

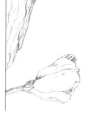

My Risen Lord

My risen Lord, I feel thy strong protection;
I see thee stand among the graves today;
"I am the Way, the Life, the Resurrection,"
I hear thee say.

And all the burdens I have sadly carried
Grow light as blossoms on an April day;
My cross becomes a staff, I journey gladly
This Easter day.

—*Author Unknown*

Restoration

Almighty God,
who through the death of your Son
has destroyed sin and death,
and by his Resurrection
has restored innocence
and everlasting life,
that we may be delivered
from the dominion of the devil,
and our mortal bodies
raised up from the dead:

Grant that we may confidently
and whole-heartedly believe this,
and, finally, with your saints,
share in the joyful resurrection
of the just;
through the same Jesus Christ,
your Son,
our Lord.

—*Martin Luther*

Let Us Rejoice

O God,
who by your One and only Son
has overcome death
and opened to us
the gate of everlasting life;

Grant, we pray,
that those who have been redeemed
by his Passion
may rejoice
in his Resurrection,
through the same Christ
our Lord.

—from the Gelasian Sacramentary

Come to Our Table

Lord, you clothe the lilies,
you feed the birds of the sky,
you lead the lambs to pasture,
and the deer to the waterside.

You multiplied loaves and fishes,
and changed the water to wine;
come to our table as giver,
and as our guest to dine.

—*Author Unknown*

Enter, O Lord

Enter, O Lord, enter this home
and bless each of us one by one
and also bless our loved ones.
Grant that we enjoy the fruits
of your redemptive peace.
With a blessed glance
deliver anything that might harm us.

Shower your divine grace
over each of us that we might share
this bread without sorrow.
With your power, Lord, free us
from anything that might hurt us
in mind, soul, and body.
Amen.

—*Sister Judith Marie Saenz*

Thanks Be to Thee

Thanks be to thee,
O Lord Jesus Christ,
for all the benefits
which thou hast given us,
for all the pains and insults
which thou hast borne for us.

O most merciful Redeemer,
friend, and brother,
may we know thee more clearly,
love thee more dearly,
and follow thee more nearly,
for thine own sake.

—Saint Richard of Chichester

My Easter Wish

May the glad dawn
Of Easter morn
Bring joy to thee.

May the calm eve
Of Easter leave
A peace divine with thee.

May Easter night,
On thine heart write,
O Christ, I live for Thee.

—*Author Unknown*

PRAYERS FOR THE
EASTER SEASON

I know that my redeemer liveth,

and that he shall stand

at the latter day

upon the earth. . . .

— Job 19:25

In Praise and Service

Make a joyful noise
unto the Lord, all ye lands.
Serve the Lord with gladness:
come before his presence with singing.
Know ye that the Lord he is God:
it is he that hath made us,
and not we ourselves;
we are his people,
and the sheep of his pasture.
Enter into his gates with thanksgiving,
and into his courts with praise:
be thankful unto him,
and bless his name.
For the Lord is good;
his mercy is everlasting;
and his truth endureth to all generations.

—Psalm 100

Prayer to Serve

Almighty Father,
who hast given
thine only Son
to die for our sins,
and to rise again
for our justification;
Grant us so to
put away the leaven
of malice and wickedness,
that we may always serve thee
in pureness of living and truth;
through the merits of the same
thy Son Jesus Christ
our Lord.
Amen.

—from the Book of Common Prayer

Immanuel's Praise

Hail, thou once despised Jesus!
Hail, thou Galilean King!
Who didst suffer to release us;
Who didst free salvation bring:
Hail, thou universal Saviour,
Who hast borne our sin and shame!
By whose merits we find favor;
Life is given through thy name.

Paschal Lamb, by God appointed,
All our sins were on thee laid;
By almighty Love appointed,
Thou hast full atonement made:
Every sin may be forgiven
Through the virtue of thy blood;
Opened is the gate of heaven;
Peace is made 'twixt man and God.

Jesus, hail! enthroned in glory,
There forever to abide;
All the heavenly hosts adore thee,
Seated at thy Father's side:

There for sinners thou art pleading:
"Spare them yet another year";
Thou for saints art interceding,
Till in glory they appear.

Worship, honor, power, and blessing,
Christ is worthy to receive;
Loudest praises, without ceasing,
Meet it is for us to give.
Help, ye bright angelic spirits!
Bring your sweetest, noblest lays!
Help to sing our Jesus' merits;
Help to chant Immanuel's praise.

—John Bakewell

Teach Us, Lord

Teach us, Lord,

To serve you as you deserve,

To give and not to count the cost,

To fight and not to heed the wounds,

To toil and not to seek for rest,

To labor and not to ask for any reward

Save that of knowing that we do your will.

Amen.

—Ignatius of Loyola

Christ's Hands

Christ has no body
now on earth but yours,
no hands but yours,
no feet but yours.
Yours are the eyes through which
He is to look out
Christ's compassion to the world;
Yours are the feet with which
He is to go about doing good;
Yours are the hands with which
He is to bless men now.

—*Saint Teresa of Ávila*

Prayer for Grace

Almighty God,
who has given thine only Son
to be unto us both a sacrifice for sin,
and also an example of godly life;
Give us grace that we may always
most thankfully receive
his inestimable benefit,
and also daily endeavour ourselves
to follow the blessed steps
of his most holy life;
through the same thy Son
Jesus Christ our Lord.
Amen.

—Collect for the Second Sunday after Easter

Almighty God

Almighty and most merciful God,
who hast given us a new commandment
that we should love one another,
give us also grace that we may fulfill it.
Make us gentle,
courteous, and forbearing.
Direct our lives
so that we may look
to the good of others
in word and deed.
And hallow all our friendships
by the blessing of thy spirit;
for his sake who loved us
and gave himself for us,
Jesus Christ our Lord.

—Bishop Brooke Foss Westcott

The Easter Light

O Lord God, our Father,
you are the light
that can never be put out;
and now you give us a light
that shall drive away
all darkness.
You are love
without coldness,
and you have given us
such warmth in our hearts
that we can love
all whom we meet.
You are the life
that defies death,
and you have opened for us
the way that leads
to eternal life.
None of us
is a great Christian;
we are all humble and ordinary.
But your grace
is enough for us.

Arouse in us
that small degree of joy
and thankfulness
of which we are capable,
to the timid faith
which we can muster,
to the cautious obedience
which we cannot refuse,
and thus to the wholeness of life
which you have prepared
for all of us
through the death
and Resurrection of your Son.
Do not allow any of us
to remain apathetic
or indifferent to the
wondrous glory of Easter,
but let the light of our risen Lord
reach every corner of our dull hearts.

—*Karl Barth*

O Lord, Support Us

O Lord,
support us all the day long,
until the shadows lengthen,
and the evening comes,
and the busy world is hushed,
and the fever of life is over,
and our work is done.
Then, Lord, in your mercy,
grant us a safe lodging
and a holy rest and peace
at last through Jesus Christ our Lord.
Amen.

—John Henry

For Faith

O God,
we give thanks that your Son,
Jesus Christ,
who has shared our earthly life,
has now ascended
to prepare our heavenly life.
Grant that,
through coming to know him
by faith on earth,
we may come to know him
by sight in heaven.

—from the Gelasian Sacramentary

Ascension Day

Grant, we beseech thee,
almighty God,
that like as we do believe
thy only begotten Son
our Lord Jesus Christ
to have ascended
into the heavens;
so we may also
in heart and mind
thither ascend,
and with him continually dwell,
who liveth and reigneth
with thee and the Holy Ghost,
one God,
world without end.

—from the Book of Common Prayer

I Love Thee

I love thee, I love thee,
I love thee, my Lord;
I love thee, my Saviour,
I love thee, my God;
I love thee, I love thee,
And that thou dost know:
But how much I love thee
My actions will show.

O Jesus, my Saviour,
With thee I am blest,
My life and salvation,
My joy and my rest:
Thy name be my theme,
And thy love be my song;
Thy grace shall inspire
My heart and my tongue.

—*Author Unknown*

At Pentecost

Good Jesu, fountain of love:
fill me with thy love,
Absorb me into thy love,
compass me with thy love,
That I may see all things
in the light of thy love,
Receive all things
as tokens of thy love,
Speak of all things
in words breathing of thy love,
Win through thy love
others to thy love,
Be kindled, day by day,
with a new glow of thy love,
Until I be fitted to enter
into thine everlasting love,
To adore thy love
and love to adore thee,
My God and my all.
Even so, come, Lord Jesu!

—E. B. Pusey

Giver of Life

Holy Spirit,
the life that gives life,
You are the cause
  of all movement;
You are the breath
  of all creatures;
You are the salve
  that purifies our souls;
You are the fire
  that warms our hearts;
You are the light
  that guides our feet.
Let all the world praise you.

—Saint Hildegard von Bingen

Renewing Pentecost

Be pleased to visit your church
with the Holy Spirit.
Renew the day of Pentecost
in our midst;
and in the midst
of all gatherings of your people,
may there come
the downfall of the holy fire,
the uprising of the heavenly wind.
May matters that are now slow and dead
become quick and full of life,
and may the Lord Jesus Christ
be exalted in the midst of his church
which is his fullness—
"the fullness of him that filleth all in all."
May multitudes be converted;
may they come flocking to Christ
with holy eagerness to find in him
a refuge as the doves
fly to their dovecotes.

—*Charles H. Spurgeon*

Prayer for Charity

O Lord,
which dost teach us
that all our doings
without charity
are worth nothing:
send the Holy Ghost,
and pour into our heart
that most excellent gift of charity,
the very bond
of peace and all virtues,
without the which,
whosoever liveth
is counted dead before thee:
Grant this, for thy only son
Jesus Christ's sake.

—from the Book of Common Prayer

Author Index

Title Index